Bent Back Tongue

Caitlin Press Inc.
3375 Ponderosa Way
Qualicum Beach, BC V9K 2J8
www.caitlin-press.com

Cover design by Vici Johnstone
Cover artwork by Tania Willard
Text design by Sarah Corsie
Edited by Sarah de Leeuw
Printed in Canada

Caitlin Press Inc. acknowledges financial support from the Government of
Canada and the Canada Council for the Arts, and the Province of British
Columbia through the British Columbia Arts Council and the Book
Publisher's Tax Credit.

Library and Archives Canada Cataloguing in Publication

Bent back tongue : poems / Garry Gottfriedson.
Gottfriedson, Garry, author.
Canadiana 20220227640 | ISBN 9781773860961 (softcover)
LCGFT: Poetry.
LCC PS8563.O8388 B46 2022 | DDC C811/.6—dc23

BENT BACK TONGUE

POEMS BY
GARRY GOTTFRIEDSON

Caitlin Press 2022

This book is dedicated to
the murdered and missing men across this country.

Contents

Canada Day, July 1st, 2021

Canada, you have claimed this July day
to boast the birth of colonial takeover
a perpetual death warrant for my people
and a day in which you have held
your own citizens in scorn
when in fact, they are blameless
to your contempt and cover-ups
and bear your sins

tell me how can I celebrate
what arose from within the deep
corners of your mind
to wordsmith the Indian Act
policies of
decimation
annihilation
degradation
and starvation

I have 215 reasons
to be skeptical of your contributions
the price of their last breathes
at the hands of church and state
your residential school legacy of
child abduction
sodomy
rape
torture
and murder

to celebrate
your colonial birthday is an acknowledgement
that their lives and mine
were not a high enough price
to appease your ghastly desire
to abuse our bodies at your will
then use our blood as ink
to write your white paper policy

we will not admit defeat
under those circumstances
because those 215 ancestral bones won't allow
the river-songs still flowing
in my blood to die so easily
nor will they permit
the graveyards in my heart to enter rage

instead they whisper
from the orchards
"they have found us"
and I share that joy
and the newfound courage
to use my voice to thank
my ancestors and awakened citizens
breaking your shame
running for the dead
riding and driving in solidarity
the kind-heartedness of Sikh and other
strangers shedding tears with us
reminding us of this simple word
tsqelmucwílc— "I have returned to being human"
and for this, I celebrate

Thrive

stars beaming
from far off unknowns
brilliant in a nocturnal sky
reaching soul
shining words
from deep love places
illuminating an old river path
onwards towards a calling den
where hearts slow down in winter
to retreat
to return
to hibernate
a resting place
a dream place
a starvation place
where all things pure and simple
thrive in truth
a body of ancestral kin
easing their way
over rock skeletons
feeding movement
swimming in blood memory
through darkness
a sparkle, a small simple sparkle
beaming life
defying death

Land and Language

written on rock
taught through oral pastime
our language is old
it was born
from the land, this land—Secwepemcúlecw
the reverberations
rumbling from sky to mountaintops
into our throats formed words
creating Secwepemctsín
streaming from the sky
touching earth
reaching our souls
melting glacier tears
weeping
forming rivers
and our hearts released
sounds of land and language

R Tmicw-kt ell Xqwélten-kt

tsqeẏ ri7 ne scenc
tselxewílcste tems q̓7e7st.s
r xqeltén-kt tskul te tmicw
ˈyi7éne r tmicw - Secwepemcúlecw
ell qeqnímete r secpéwt te tkmesq̓t
tkten skwelkwélt-uy
te sq̓wmellqwélt.s-kuc kult r seqwlút
m- secwepemctseném-et
stek te tkmesq̓t
kétes r tmicw
tskitses r stelsqélecwes
míxwes r skwelkwelt-uy r skwcust.s
cc r ts7úmes
kult r setétkwe
kellekstméte r púsme-kt
m-qeqnímete r tmicw ell xqwélten-kt

14

Ink on Paper

he tells me
he has read my poetry
delved into it
repeatedly
believes
he knows
the secrets of my heart

he tells me
he has mingled in my metaphors
socializing with those tricksters in diction
imagining
that he is Koyoti himself,
crawling
in and out of my skin
howling in my silence

he tells me
he has bathed in my images
washing
himself with used textures
using the same bark
that I used to scrub my body with
the grit peeled away wetly, hauntingly
infatuated with the sap of trees in my words

he tells me
he has heard each tone
resonating from my voice
understands
my deep growls
can taste the pine pitch
sticking to my tongue
devouring my sounds

he tells me
he has a man-crush on me
wants to eat my words
wants to crawl into my bed

whispering
midnight sounds
he wants that magic touch
because of my poetry

I tell him
perhaps
he mis(s)-understands me
that my poetry is second-hand information
once it leaves my mind
and what the eye perceives is interpretive
but really, it is only ink on paper

Brown Man

a brown man slipping
white without purpose
can't whiten his race

obsession is an extraordinary risk
because decimation
angers other brown brothers

it is genuine departure of the self
attempting to be something
you are not

I can accept
you for the man you are
if you are true to yourself

but remember
being born brown
is the privilege

Men Like Me

my body speaks of men like me
compressed and contained
conditioned by stereotypes
shaped by white privilege
chosen to be someone's
trashy love story
still carting a stoic Indian inside
kicking up dust on rez roads
loving the scent of earth after it rains
or strutting our stuff along Robson St
Vancouver's banana republic district
forever straddling two worlds

still, we are handsome savages
fulfilling fantasies
hidden from the moon's beam
shining bear-like eyes
still knowing we are not elite enough
to sit centre in the Blue Water Café on Hamilton St
in the light of day

we all know our ranks in society
Indian pride is knowing
we love ourselves
enough to stand our ground
despite ignorance
but knowing
we are never noble enough to sport
our images on centre stage
definitely not on the queen's currency
no matter how much we have
contributed to this country and to the world

instead, we have become
what others have forced us to be
locked into public policy and pleasure
dangerously drifting from the red earth
hardly in touch with Granny's soft skin
becoming deaf to Grampa's stories

sometimes barely remembering
we were born with bruises and blood
that we were born naked
that we were born brown
that our parents walked
hunched over
along a similar path a generation before us
weighted down with a queen's victory
the woman who never knew her own children
who had no hand in raising them

but we never forgot the lessons
our ancestors taught us
their words inked in our bones
our own backs bent heavy
our iron hearts breaking gracefully
seven generations at a time
notwithstanding this, we give
meaning to something more than ourselves
yet, the weight of our travels stretches our limbs
carves ruts in our faces that tell it all
our spines carry ghosts
protruding from our skins
and there are graveyards
caving in on our throats
still, feeble throaty songs reach beyond us

our growls are that of our ancestors
mumbling English atrocities
fighting the savages
who stripped us
of our mother-tongues
the swelling tongues of foreigners
calculating our futures with precision

we fumble to explain this
when we look into the eyes of our children
hiding shame
and forever at war

yet, we love this land
until our bodies rot
bearing it in our children's hearts

true, we have been beaten
and bent into something beautiful
our voices rumbling
thunder from graves
but we can still taste
rain streaming from our souls
so strong is our will to live
we are alive
we are alive
and we speak for men like me

Bent Back Tongue

the mind creates
riots of its own
not seeing beyond one's self

imagine a bent back tongue
reaching backbone purposefully
driving swords into the spine

this is called separation
of word and love
consider this

there is no gulping back
words impulsive or not
when the tongue is an angry weapon

I know this well
and turn back to us
reflecting

Conversations

silence is awkward peacefulness
when you are alone in conversation
the space between us buzzing

I stare out the window
sip water and whisky
it is morning

a hummingbird catches my eye
I watch it drink sweet nectar
before it takes flight

it is all memory now
things left unsaid
birds in flight

breaking hearts
is personal after all
was there a better choice?

Broken Butterflies

there is something desolate
about sleepy afternoons
staring at broken butterflies
homeless in bodies, like mine

I can't be the only one
half-awake and adrift
with a bible in hand
but an atheist at heart

realization is cruel
witnessing atrocity is worse
even the sound of fractured wings
triggers regret

Four Is a Sacred Number

1)
my thin chest flames blue
bankrupt apologies hatch
silence fills the room

2)
thorns snuggled inside
a sweaty bed burning thin
I am wide awake

3)
no blood to speak of
there are holes in my backside
a fly buzzes over

4)
graveyards are forever
wild roses drop petals at night
I am alive still

Livestreaming in Arequipa, Peru (2019)

1)
wandering cobblestone streets in Arequipa
timeworn and heavy with routine, over centuries
leading paths to the plaza
where internal wars remain
amidst whitewashed structures

2)
meandering among the robotic descendants
of colonial aristocrats and Indigenous peoples
is an incredible love story of survival
a one-sided affair prevalent
and waiting for brave truth-seekers
to ask questions flung to the new world

3)
"where does loyalty fit?" the poet asks
beaming beautifully
amid the ragged-eyed
portraits of long-gone thieves
hanging silently from palace walls
watching with dead eyes
and staring back
questions of their own
clinging to crumbling identity
slicing a piece of their lives away
for the glory of spain

4)
"we have seen it all with new-born eyes"
replies the clueless foreigner

5)
"here this," the reply
it is not easy to forget
hounds dog-trotting
out of the belly of spanish ships
belly crawling onto the land
hunger eating their marrow
all for a spanish queen

6)
mouths dry of spit
and hearts full of bullets
shooting from parched souls
500 years of gunpowder
branding lessons
deeply into Indigenous bones and eyes,
the realization is astounding

7)
this is history
this is now

8)
the spanish flag proudly wagers
genocide—even to this day

9)
and along the way, yipping dogs bark at invisible death
still lurking in streets
still tromping a path to the plaza
the air is full of poetry and questions
deeply rooted in Quechua soul

10)
today, poetry lovers gather
clinging and crawling along structures
filling palace chambers with aching bodies
sitting on wooden chairs
listening to the sound of shattering hearts
contemplating recurrences
expressed in lyrical perfection

11)
their poetry shifts further south
livestreaming modern history
retelling of eyes bursting
gold and blood
sweating and throbbing
desires between visitors' legs centuries old

12)
but spain is not what it used to be
transformation is spain's karma
glory is the tiny blue spark of ancient souls
beckoning the return of indigeneity
blossoming through music and poetry

13)
Mapuche cousins rise in the south
marching a heavy migration
pure and ancient
the dead are singing war songs
to drag down godoy's head
and hang it from the arm and pride of Mapuche civilization

14)
it is coming
it is coming

15)
the wind fights
relentlessly in the squalls of change
conquistadors crumble in the streets
for *the bloody pacification of the Mapuche*
heartland has twisted itself inside out
this is Mapuche destiny
this is solidarity
rising like heatwaves over the land
insulting spaniards' machoism
retaliation is to gouge out an eye
but this will not blind freedom
Indigenous people will not falter
in their quest to reclaim themselves

16)
and I watch, we all watch
livestreaming in Arequipa

On This Side of Heaven

the sun sets
on this side of heaven

beams stream through
stained glass windows

I am on my knees
in doubtful prayer

the rays piercing my soul
this church is empty

Ugly

some people are
afraid of ugly
ugly people
ugly words
I am ugly
my poetry is ugly

ugly priests drilled
ugly into our beauty
anointed us ugly
to ensure ugly secrets
were an act of contrition

my love seeks
beauty
beyond ugly

Cactus and Wild Roses

the blue ceiling of sky
sprawls the rugged landscape
over our homelands
it can change its colours anytime
some things are predictable, others are not
but transformation is constant
a wave of life and death in all forms
rolling over centuries of customs
built upon the dust of ancestors
enticed by the old language of land
the desire to thrive
the art of living
breaths of fresh air
pure, untainted food
giving meaning to tribes
marking borders of territories
protecting the resources within
the hearts and will of people
inspired by the blue sky gathering clouds
evolving into celebration
the making of ceremonies
healing ceremonies
water ceremonies
because water is life
snow and rain are lifeforces
filling the skies
nurturing the land
like the blood of our mothers
veins of streams and rivers
feeding land and all relatives
remembering all life begins in water
and this is worth fighting for

it is a fight for all people
protecting things that heal
returning bodies to pure states
remembering that sacrifices are necessary
that blood bursts and spills for great cause

like mothers who give birth
spectacular miracles
labour
for the right to breathe
bringing meaning
in defence of children
strong, healthy children
who maintain balance
in a world gone wrong
so when women stand
shoulder to shoulder
in defiance of sloppy policies
that promote ill health
and the decimation of humanity
the foreign laws that invade
the hunger growing in their bellies
remember
mothers are not to be messed with
and it is up to men to warrior up
because a man comes from her body
and he must go back
understanding her intentions
returning to the land
in search of red ochre
to paint his face with earthly power
and build buffers in defence of healthy communities
bringing with him a tribe of brothers
and new weapons
to smash wrongful acts
that disregards the pure and raw natural
beauty of the land, water, air and people
warriors must know
the lay of the land and the dictionary well
because laws are two-sided
freedom or sealed fate
health or death
silencing voices
is absolute ridicule after all

extinction is real and possible
we have seen this
colonial and government promises
exposed
between the spaces of bureaucratic teeth
nearly eradicating tribal voices and identity
the knowledge and pathways to healthy dialogue
this is not a future to leave grandchildren with
erotic and erratic settler behaviour
perpetuated
desires already charted
pathways to destruction
corralling souls
claiming watersheds
growing invasive crops
digging into the landscape
for oil and gas
for diamonds and gold
melting down idol promises
putting reserves on men and women's fingers
imprisoning them
even creating highways
for murdered and missing women and men
this is called civilization
this is called assimilation
and this is Canada's aspiration
and there is nothing healthy about it

our bones tell it all
deep within marrow
understanding
reversal is reprisal
witnessed
by land in drought
the skies dropping acid rain
transforming colour
making deserts that survive
and from the cracked skin of land and hearts
cactus and wild roses thrive

even grow between the land
filled with bone-dust and love
inducing centuries of labour
screaming out in pain
bursting into joyful song
for tribal identities and rights to endure
and amid it all, the hovering of scab policies
like dc scott's Indian Act
the ratification for death or assimilation
the conversation must be on equal terms
the words must hold meaning to and from
revenge is not the answer
if we are to reverse this state
it is not about assimilation
one culture over another
it is about recognizing
the brilliance in all peoples
but it will surely be a death warrant
should ethnocentric views dominate
simply, it is a war of worldviews
we are alive amid ultimate sins

why not return to the desire to thrive?

L.O.L.

the teepee door flips
wide open
headed straight
for the powwow trail
snag'n lane is a free-for-all
love path
talking fingers
texting via snap chat
gets the guys there
but what ever happened to smoke signals?

silly boys!

Climate Change

are we in dawn?
or are we in dusk?

world ablaze
forests turning to ash
burning holes in the sky
fires singeing heaven
dense smoky orange
obliterating the blue beyond
dragging a smoke net
across the land
slow and thick
as oil spills

our eyes clouded grey
we can't see the destruction
clear as it may be
we can't see
the simplicity of things
as they should be
something is wrong

are we in dawn?
or are we in dusk?

the sky snarls
taking in deep breaths
holding them dearly
desiring a clear path to heaven
despite our lungs charred
and voices barely audible
clearing our throats of graveyards
prayers crackle into grumbles
the mere desperation for faith

life weighed down
our skins weighed down
our hearts weighed down
bullied by the trumps in the world

dragging
capitalistic soot to our graves
the burden is immense
the stakes are high
this is an ugly legacy
for our grandchildren

are we in dawn?
or are we in dusk?

murky shades of thought
imbalanced ideology
insensibility
when sensibility is most needed
there is no time
to be drunk, stoned nor idle
worry and fear worn in
the deep crevasses of our minds
still, there is idleness
still, escapism is the drug
drying out our mouths
still, whisky bullets is the 'go-to' for numbing
still, we move about daily routines
stuffing bellies full at McDonalds
honking horns in line-ups at Starbucks drive-throughs
still, flicking cigarette butts from car windows
still mindless
scattering thoughts
clogged minds
losing track of the day
losing track of time

are we in dawn?
or are we in dusk?

we are lost for solutions
confused in chaos
voiceless in voting
refocus calls for action

unifying is arduous
we all face common cause
common enemies
governments for the rich
prisons for the poor
oppressive policies
political bullies
children killing children
alternatives seem unreachable
apathetic citizens
while the land swelters
avalanches of ash
burying life
heavy grime
clinging to our bones
to our eyes
we don't see
value in protests
residential school protests
murder protests
suicide protests
drug overdose protests
loss of hope protests
pipeline protests
and other possible devastation protests
that need an army of voice warriors
that need an army of land warriors
that need an army of water warriors
that need an army of firefighters
to awaken a saddened world

are we in dawn?
or are we in dusk?

people are wailing in darkness
grannies and grandpas crying soot
women fighting with no men to back them up
the National or CNN doesn't show this on prime time
prime ministers and presidents are hedonistic

they speak to appease
addicts of greed
centuries of pure greed
bred and evolved into white privilege
industrial revolution descendants
still breeding cha-ching, cha-ching
dollar signs tattooed in their corneas
world classification, world devastation
forged from Victoria's crown
burning our forests down
and leaving us with questions

are we in dawn?
or are we in dusk?

Blackhole

a blackhole
atmospheric mass
travelling
orbits shift
at the weight of space
bursting
in all directions

we only see
the night sky
or selected things
humans can collect
or disregard
when usefulness
centres around numbers

but where do
our real concerns go?
deep within
the body's sphere-cape
scientists don't have
a metric scale at hand
to calculate human collision

Mongrels

for Robin, Joanne and Vi

mongrels prowl
my matriarch's doorstep

she smells them coming
waits silently

she knows the familiar
sound of bitches barking

panting mouths
drooling on the hunger hunt

leaving their bite marks
like tombstones

but she is solid fearlessness
my matriarch, my Violet

Graves

there are unmarked tombstones
jetting from sunset horizons

metamorphoses in bloom
signs that things could be unalike

edging flat flowers of adoration
dry sinking into a spring sun

and at the graveyard corridors
magpies chatter in black and white

damning sad-eyed kin
heads bowed in damnation

hearts stuck in throats
realizing remorse in living memory

willing to let go is not so easy
the crickets will still weep at night

rain will nurture the land tomorrow
and more violets will grow in the days to come

summer's approach bares
a sister's beauty forevermore

but the other one wishing death upon her own kin
awaits her arrival at the grave alone

a casket heavy with stubborn regrets
a lesson for many to decide well

Lethal

I believed in my family once
that unity was blood-binding

that no matter the enemy
our family would overcome

but when blood turns rancid
there is nothing left

but rotting corpses
dead relatives walking

all it takes is a taste of jealousy
greed and narcissism

to inject the death sentence
and when the first born does this

it is lethal
and there is nothing left to believe in

Other Secrets

I study your lament
an examination of convictions
extraordinary illusions

I am amazed
you have convinced yourself
to leave out the juicy details

you thought I was too young
to remember the other secrets
wrinkling your face

but intuitively, you know
I didn't believe your musings
yet, you couldn't stop yourself

like aging without wisdom
is an old person's calamity
some people just grow old stupid

with mouths full of dirty words
mumbling
unforgivable things

so think about this
love can never be begged back
once it is destroyed

so sad
you made
that choice...

Flint-chipped

swift and restless
poetry

arrow straight
stanzas

shooting
multi-meanings

targeting
poetry lovers or others

privileged ears or not
privileged lives or not

flint-chipped imagery
weakens the apology

or entices
glee

bleeding out
blue words

natural openness
blueprints either way

like mixed-blood love
reality, not fantasy

it tingles alluring aches
joy or disappointment

no more
soaring eagle poems

winged
in flight

but flying
nevertheless

sparrow poems
sharp and diving

relentless
with intent

and then joy
yes, joy

thighs full and warm
hearts frantic

speaking poetry
perhaps, lusty love poems

or even lost identity
searching out place poems

searching
out peace poems

reading
into things is vital

but settling
for whom ever is risky

people
misconstrue things easily

poetry
is a trickster

metaphors
change

meaning
duality exists

especially
in multi-cultural societies

choosing
can be confusing

knowing
is substantial enough

people
endlessly search

believe
in saviors

believe
their high price has saved them

believe
that Indigenous folk have answers

some do
but many don't

and promote pan-Indian love
spinning medicine wheel misfortune

something more real
is needed for the long haul

craving
tonto and lone ranger love won't do

it is shockingly wicked
it is shockingly stupid

colliding with ice
cool the engine down, baby

disenchanting or enchanting
realizations

not a low battery
but fully charged

not an act of God
something deeper

the rush is coming
calling all angels

with soft teeth
and broken wings

or wicked skeptics
mouths full of body love

the air is heavy
with movement

maybe rain
maybe snow

it is tough to fly
weighed down

desperation is not a cure
but poetry helps

Dismantling

dismantling white privilege
one brain at a time
is reclaiming the Indigenous self

in fact, it is colonizing the colonizers
and it is a dirty job
scrubbing out toilet bowls

a Ph.D. is not needed
for common sense nor to see
things as they are

even the starkness of white
policy will be defied and defeated
for it is an act of brown privilege

that's what artists are for
it is why writers have voice
and it is called 'conscience'

so while painting ancestral presence
the brush is the bullet
the keyboard types political poetic policies

and now the transformation begins
→ get over it ←

Imagine That!

roaming the black streets
slopping down beers
when the game ends
mouths full of Corona
leaking
drunk
conversation
spilling onto the streets

"raise your bottle bro!"
"I am a man-whore."

dislodging fear
timbering in
voiceless anarchy
but let us toast to all the dead loves
who made ghosts of us
staked to white privilege
who made our existence ugly
who thought their armour
was a high prize to save themselves
and who make our love
sinful acts

imagine that!

it is time
it is time
to examine the walking dead
the heartless nature of man
the women who hate men
the child who dies
an overdose death
the orphans from the 60s scoop
the day scholar addicts
the residential school drunks
and the pope-forgiven priests and nuns
excused from hell

imagine that!

the stroke of the queen's pen
made them mercenaries
while our tired and frail grannies wailed
atop of mountains
when the snows dissolved
to set fiery heatwaves
to soften the earth
so that avalanche lilies could sprout
and sprout they did
hearing our life-givers
hearts break in prayer
like thunder cracking
begging the Creator
to give might to those
one little
two little
three little
… ten little
Indian children barely alive
but surviving enough
to give reason for research

imagine that!

so let us call upon
our dead loves and researchers
to consult and conduct findings
better yet, let us delve into the books ourselves
digging deep within our own worldviews
to buckle the old boys club
and find logic
worthy to convince
pessimistic wrong-doers
that the riot has bled
drunkards
flooding
the dark corners in the streets
weighed down with the remnants of our whoring days
and dragging skeletons upon our backs

into university corridors
asking questions
seeking answers
picking up the pen
to write poetry or plays or films or novels
in search of the perfect answer
to resurrect the perfect Indian
obedient as a british wife
loyal as an orphan child
pretty as a Gucci boy
but brilliant as is our right

imagine that!

cast away
cast away
the drunk and stoned
drunk and stoned
talking drunk
talking sober
smashing beer bottles
encompassing our agony
in each grain of glass sand
not to mention our resilience
and resistance to colonial influence
soul strong enough to
flush away those pills
down a toilet's abyss
and zipping up our pants
burying the drought in our hearts
forgetting it all
forgetting it all
replenishing our dry depths
with blood once more

imagine that!

it is all about action now
live streaming

smart boards
bayonets in our minds
counting coup in accounting classes
staring into the eyes
of privileged white men
towing in allies
from every geometric angle
writing perfectly persuasive papers
ready to be stacked
on newly built shelves on parliament hill
that will redress Canada's dirty history
forcing another useless public apology
and providing new meaning to truth
never mind reconciliation
there is something beautifully
wrong when the conquered fade
drastically wrong!
and there is something tragically
liberating when lilies bloom

imagine that!

Sometimes

sometimes I am afraid
of the sky giving birth
to a new day, I want to hide
under a blanket of forever night

sometimes I see things
when I don't want to
like prayers falling from the sky
shattering on pavement
the images of beaten-down paths before me

sometimes I witness
needles protruding from the arms of men
lost and disinterested
in their own natural spirit
and running from their own gifts

sometimes I am tired
of repeatedly having to justify my skin
the way my brown body moves in shadows
the way I must always have thunder in my voice
because deafness is astounding

sometimes I am weak
from fighting, my fists bleeding the mouthy debris
of defending my birthrights
for a future
and my mixed blood grandchildren

sometimes I don't want to remember
my broken heart was once loved by you

Purpose

there is something fine
about cohesive cultural constructs
building
great values
for the good of the clan
feeding souls
imagining
sustainability
for those yet to be born

our job is not done—yet

Sealed

I am epic
by number 688, for I am
the queen's legal ward
in this lifetime

I am stripped of my identity
imprisoned in my motherland
sealed by the sovereign
forever an unlawful child

I am worthless
in both pound and dollar
and expendable
at the whim of a quill

I will never have my face
imprinted on currency
nor be of white value
despite my contributions

I must always be put
in my place, reminded
that I am not good enough
even to rate myself

I pack this realization
shame is the sound
of Canadians snarling "get over it"
"I had nothing to do with it"

I know the soullessness of man
has everything to do with
decimation and abolishment
of race pure and natural

I get that freedom lives in our imaginations
imprisonment is real
it is the dead weight of breath
dropped onto paper

I tune out mumbling apologies
because truth is something to be heard
and it is so easy to believe in lies
since hearts are fragile

I relentlessly seek out
the colour of midnight blue oddly calm
awaiting
another lifetime

liberty!

The Design

gun in hand
she inks
genealogy
geography
humanity
mapping
pathways
rivers
mountains
family
ancestral stories
when the time has come
to tell the story
on living skins

Northern Lights

night steals daylight
midnight crackles
northern lights
ghosts riding bareback
humming Tea Dance song
flooding heaven with song

the star-speckled sky opens to
secretive language often misunderstood
patterns of hungry sounds
clear circles of chattering ancestors
looking down at us
promising warmth, sending laughter

crawling into our sleep
bringing dreams alive
tracing back time
when memory became a word
among the living
dreaming laughter

Tā Moko

tā moko, you awaken me
on a Secwépemc full moon
night ablaze with need
my skin remembering
the hands that tell
the story of my being
my reason for being
compelled to relieve the itch
my skin peeling black flakes
my struggling eyes
adapting to dimness
but my vivid mind
sees the man
I now call brother
the gift, the exchange
hongi, greenstone and brotherhood
constant as waves
rhythmic on the Pacific
living song
frozen in my lungs, until
the moist breath of the ocean
tempers my skin
we are brothers
north and south
bound by hemispheres
invisible lines
and the Pacific Ocean
Māori and Secwépemc
the waters, the mountains, the genealogy
nose to nose
heart to heart
I embrace you

Discussions

1)
truth is meaningless
words without heart and true soul
it is cold inside

2)
search deeply, or else
reconciliation dies
the rain is coming

3)
choking unilingual
lies create deep and dark mistrust
fall is in the air

4)
reciprocity
means bilingual discussions
the sun shines outside

Tears

winter's pearl tears
do not drop
but flutter
downward
settling upon
snowcapped mountains
building
glaciers and avalanches

spring's diamond tears
drizzle
a warning
soon the thunder will
awaken
hibernating land
a single trickle of rain
building
streams and rivers

summer's topaz tears
shimmer
off the sun's prisms
flash-dancing
over holy water
awakening the soul
to a kaleidoscope of colours, joy
and the sweet smell of earth
after a rain

autumn's ruby tears
splatter
a spectrum of beauty
before the land
sleeps
brilliance seen as heartache
when in fact
the collection of tears
is a blissful reminder
of life

Flute Songs

rugged shores booming
ocean's reoccurrence
salt in the air
sand rolls black in Pila
shaped by the sea's waves and wind
whimsical clouds
shield the sun
momentarily

this land was named for clouds

extending from earth to sky
dependent on air for life
the wind carries
the weight of clay flute songs
from shore to forest
primordial melodies
transported by heaven's breath
over oceans, forests, mountains and deserts
warm and insistent

Powwow

1)
powwow bravado
escapes his boyhood at dusk
city lights shine dull

2)
unzipped fun drums lust
her nipples invite quick hope
give him a cold beer

3)
Sagehills sings heart songs
that isn't tribal at all
its anything-goes time

4)
boys don't need flowers
just a one-night stand will do
it's a new day gone

Aotearoa

Aotearoa, there is prayer
on the beach at Piha
where I washed my heart
and arms in the salty sea

the black sands warming
my feet wandering the caves
returning to the doorway

drawn into the drumming
of whitecapped waves
I threw my head back in pure joy

the sky, the sea and this beach
alive in soulfulness
I will return to you—Aotearoa

Blocked Ears

he calls
on English sounds
to write from a place
no one sees, but who can
feel the chaos words can create
when they are murmured in blocked ears
or when they are sprawled across parliamentary
desktops stacked perfectly dormant awaiting another death

he uses
stones in his poetry
and the wet weight of rain
on rocks, slipping from his tongue
whispering the names of insects crawling
across his skin-scape, living beneath the heaviness
of men stomping and munching over the little lives crawling out
from depths of poetry and making of paths bound for the departing sun

Neither Poet nor Scholar

I unleash
my voice on paper
study questions
play with words

I mark
my identity on fallen trees
imagine its movements
when it had life

I am present
among my people
equally modest
astoundingly strong

I know
I am the sound of my motherland
Secwepemcúlecw
loud with colours

I am old blood
making rivers
charting paths
bringing news

I am aware
my place is humble
pure as tumbling rain
but neither poet nor scholar

Secwepemcúlecw: land of the Secwépemc

The Marae

for Graham Grayza Tipene

at the Marae in Ōrākei, you showed me
the story of stars woven
along the sky's wall, vast connections
under one sky
tracing
infinite linage and memory
"our blood," you said
patterns of light
quilting the night
immeasurable as love itself
on this side of heaven,
the voice of you is the voice of ancestors
trekking their way
to live in our skins
it was named—*Tā Moko*
charred from the edge
of fire and sorrow
our identity, our skins, our mountains, our rivers—our bloodlines
embodied in the essence
of the Marae and Tā Moko
every reason there is breath
rising in our ribs
pushing our veins
full of muscle memory
dropping a tear of pure joy
shining in the sheer silence
from where we have come
the stars and ink in summer
the pearl tears in winter
falling from the sky

we are not so different after all

Dangling

the dim light of moon
shines isolation
wallowing
near the river and rugged landscape

sagebrush and cacti heavily fill
the night long and old
with the scent of 'gone'
and I can feel it
growing
into a long night

this night growls
against my skin
it is a short space
between my brain
and the midnight breeze
only skin and bone divide it
so much can be imagined
so much can be heard
so much can dangle

the air tingles in this moment
the hair on my arms rises
because I hear Karlo Mila's poetry
dangling
inside my head
thrashing
against the walls within my soul

her words drop
drop me to my knees
stunned by her power
falling...
falling...
there are so many ways to fall
and I have fallen
for Karlo Mila's poetry

you are dangling in her stanzas
she and you
inspire me
to write blue poems
like Picasso   .
bleeding blue oil
like me
bleeding from my pen
like my lungs
coughing up your name— 'grief'

I thought I had given you up— 'grief'
wrote silly love poems— 'grief'
crumpled you up— 'grief'
sheets of dying love
grief
scattered
along the riverbanks in pools
puddles after a soothing rain
cleansing
my thoughts in the river's cold water
when the sun made way for moon
when the dim light dangled... dangled
grief

I was sure
I had nothing
more to think about
nothing more to write about
but then vowels and verbs shifted
dangled images
resurrected love before death
intense intoxication took over
tequila spinning notes into frenzied sonnets
the worm at the bottom of the bottle
formed patterns
tipping over
making waterfalls
carving ditches into my troubled face

I saw myself in the reflection
vague yellow light shimmered in the background
dangled in the glimmer of hope
barely alive
grasping a way to reject 'goodbye'
to someone who had already let go

and my voice, my dangling voice
lost in the deep blue of night
lost in the last embrace
lost in the last dangling kiss
dried and chopped up
by the wind in my head
fluttered into the dimness of moonlight

letting go... letting go
and I can feel it
I can feel all of it
deeply
dangling
dangling

Nectar

the nights belong to us
crazy, blissful consolation
wild roses strewn
across the bed
soft pink petals and thorns
rolling in the deep
earthly scents
as natural as the light of day
the backs of stems bending
ribs heaving
responding
to the whispers of bees
searching nectar
soft purring wisps
their galloping tongues
humming
travelling
wing-spread mountains
pollination in flight
raw and pure
naked in the pre-dawn

Rationale

I was never made
to bend my back to others
to become a slave to femininity or masculinity
to stoop to every woman not named wife
to cower to every man not named husband

I was never made
to bow my head to monarchs or peasants
to be apathic to governments or society
to kiss the feet of popes or devils
to be politically or religiously inept

I was never made
to be a small, small stereotype
to be only waste high to others
to have my dreams used against me
to limit the things I dream about

I was never made
to close my eyes to things worth seeing
to daydream in only shades of grey
to blink away tears when they need to be shed
to pretend the only thing worth seeing is beauty

I was never made
to be silent in a world drunk on narcissism
to imprison my tongue
to die of thirst or forget the taste of raspberries
to reject my body from becoming the storyteller

I was made to say it like it is …

Soundless

I am ready
to dispel
those living in me
because they don't know
they are dead

I have broken open
bones in my chest
snatching angst
to release you
all of you

and the world is soundless

Trepidation

my guess is that
when he walked out on you
with a bullet in his heart
and razor blades protruding from his tongue
you ran into the streets
across empty parking lots
over sharp stones in bare feet
your heart bleeding from your feet
escaping ghosts clinging to your bones

it hurts to see you like that
doubting your self-worth
and holding on too long
to something that should've
died in a parking lot years ago
perhaps you couldn't see
he didn't deserve you
and that you have more good
in your heart than he will ever have

Drunk on Poetry

I could've sworn
that was me
getting drunk on poetry

a survivor of dull re-occurrences
delving into unyielding conversations
churning circles of stubborn talk
and force-feeding my belly
full of devastation
drowning in a pond of Corona
flatly claiming calm illusions
crafted into selfish pleasure

I have never smoked
but I imagine
puffing on a menthol cigarette
smoldering blue smoke
contemplating grey thought
rising into a thin straight line
since the wind has stopped tonight

it is on nights like this
with corona in hand
and a smoke dangling
from my mouth corner
that talking to myself
barely numbs the soul
I shoulda left first without a goodbye
things mighta been different then

but I sit on a wet California eve
staring from an apartment balcony
captured by the fireflies
vivid in autumn's eye
the colour of death fluttering down
crying in my beer
emptying
what remains in my heart
begging chance
for trust once more
and getting drunk on poetry

Paper Love

paper love
a romantic escape
say what you can't

voice it on paper

a lover's leap
towards ink
and paper cuts

A Motel Made of Bones

my body is a motel
made of bones

filling space
with bare necessities

this is where I am
removed from home

unlocking my heart
when no one is watching

showering away the blues
and spellbound by the sky

building new clouds
the days are never the same

today, I see a morning-dove
snatched from flight

its breaking voice fading
between heaven and earth

crows are vicious
my escape is temporary

I return to myself
looking straight into mirrors

that morning-dove, that crow
belongs to me

I lay down
on a bed where many others have slept

thinking of us
interrupted by stark sounds

an old dog barks outside
all dogs have their time

sometimes, there is nothing
tangible in sounds or thought

not even a dog in a dead mind slump
those are muffling thoughts

questions with no answers
or answers with blunt replies

realization is nasty, yet
the physical presence of things is factual

this room is messy
clothes strewn over chairs

whisky splattered
the glass is half full

hangovers are real
and science has not discovered a cure

it is a new day though
daylight finds its way through the curtains

perhaps a good cup of coffee
will untangle birds in flight

speckled against
the snowy wings of mountains

beyond this space
mountains are heavy with excuses

skinning my mind
bearing sober truth

I tidy up the mess
sip fresh coffee

and for a moment, watch electric blue
snake dance across the sky

thinking about yesterday's dog barking
trapped in its den

coffee drips from its rim
cold sound of silence

dividing the light
a reminder that things change—even die

but now, it is time to pack up
and check out near noon

Sunset

bones framing
a love story in sunset

doves and sparrows
hovering

marrow deep
risks

real enough
to write poetry about

think on this
deeply

the red sun slants westward
tucking itself into night

where fragile birds in flight
wing themselves into nightfall

Turn on the Lights, Baby

some people think
he's a street hound
far removed from the dirt
roads meandering on his remote rez
alive all night long
in love with the night
in love with himself
lazy in dawn's expanse

some people murmur in corners
or sit around staff room tables
gossiping about his skid-row mouth
his brown tongue boom booming
sexy rez licks
a lingo in itself
insulting
those standing too close

some people secretly crave
trashy love
get turned on by his dirty talk
or the way feet fumble
onward home with him
crawling into his glass teepee
and making up their own stories

some people flirt with their eyes
offers to entice an embrace
want his tongue
want to be his unzipped stranger
passing through the threshold
mouthing drunk sounds
"turn off the lights, baby"
flickering in a rez man's landscape

some people think he needs
the dim back porch light on
to see things as they are
but things are hard to see

when one is too drunk on himself
while others are in it to count coup
perhaps, they aren't so sober after all

some people don't know his name
and it doesn't matter anyway
his name is alive at home on the rez
and this is when he needs
the warmth of the sun
to cleanse left-over shadows
slowly bleeding and webbing across
the sky of his darkened bedroom
most have never been in those places
because they are homeless and nameless
wandering the loneliness of downtowns

some people think only of his shortfalls
casting limitations on who they are
never experiencing anything other than privilege
but instinctively know his capabilities
extend far beyond hunter and prey
deploring their own weaknesses
knowing they will become prey
if they are not careful
weakening under the words "let's do it"
obsessive undertones
leading a path from his neck to his groin
bringing alive their dull existence

some people assume too much
forget he has a child's heart
in a man's body, "cruel!" he thinks
narrowing his imagination
to the white sounds in the city
macho twerking as proof
that experience outweighs hedonism
flushing sweaty pitter patters body wide
primitive growls from deep forests
and city sirens slashing assumptions

some people imagine
he lives in the sun
even when the sky boils a storm
bringing on the grey
alerting the dark-skinned angels
laughing out loudly
taunting
ridiculing
misjudging
such a tragic comedy

"turn on the lights, baby"

Snow Tracks

I heard my lover's heart
singing in a January storm

breathing
becomes ceremony in mid-winter

ice-covered songs
sealed beneath the glass frame

through the ice crystals
framing the window

I discover snow tracks
leading to warmer places

but my tongue is frozen
sitting idle until spring

Wild Fires

small smoke smoldering
beneath the core of things

a hot heart buried in ash
the cut sky promises rain

and so the wait begins
for the days to change colour, like autumn

Suitcase Memories

a man's name ties belly knots
deep within the gut
it's not really the butterfly-feeling kind
the kind that makes a lover giggle
it's the long-gone suitcase memory kind
packed full of madness and need

his conquests are swift dirty thoughts
not always thinking with the right head
and his intuition is not always right
treating others well is the better option
but sometimes men forget that
also, his name is really all he has

N-O

because I manned-up
timbering a flat 'no'
a simple two letter word N – O
making a man of me
transformative 'no'
'no' a word of peace
'no' a word of war
'no' for strategy
'no' to standing ground
'no' to everything right
'no' to everything wrong
understanding 'no'

with that simple two letter word N-O
destruction to salvation
lay on a simple path ahead of me
and I offered honesty
but perhaps, my straightforwardness
spiked my hands to the edge of stars
bleeding out the shine within
my sides draining broken promises to myself
and all that lived within me
flowing from a world in which stars thrive
bending my tongue into your name
with renewed life
gasping breath
giving back
the last syllable of you without anger
finally throwing your name to the sky
strewn along the milky way

because I had to crawl inward
when I saw you in his smile
repeating the word 'no'
I plucked every piece of you out of my ribs
scattered torn petals along the roadside
leaving a trail of words leading nowhere
there is nothing rational about love

it is clumsy and blissful
a raw road to travel

dispersed with bits and pieces of each other

it takes courage
seeing things as they are
comfort is in the small
things we build around ourselves
routines between couples
defined movements between bodies and souls
realizations men thrive in freedom

because when I stood before you
voicing that astounding word 'no'
for all the men who have said 'no'
before me without shame
my world opened without guilt
deliberate and intentional understanding
that when a man says 'no'
it is often heavy to carry
even for the right reasons
and he will carry it alone
beneath the canopy of starlit nights
or down freeways leading to unassuming pathways
following him into the spaces he recreates
knowing no one may claim his autonomy
so, I am not ashamed nor fearful
to call things as they are

because I manned-up
timbering a flat 'no'
a simple two letter word N – O
making a man of me
transformative 'no'
'no' a word of peace
'no' a word of war
'no' for strategy
'no' to standing ground
'no' to everything right
'no' to everything wrong
understanding 'no'

Your Name Drops

skies promise grey
rain is soft this morning
I hear your name drop

Floating

you are in this obscure space
floating in the back of my mind

it is neither love nor desire
just the presence of two

spirits intertwined in lost flight
it is inessential to reach out to you

even though, I have nothing to offer
that may fill your soul

accept these poetic words
drained from silent places

to write
in memory of you

Cruel Illusion

cancer is lethal misery
an exaggeration for hopefulness

tyranny of the disallowed
bloated with self-importance

a cruel illusion
and silence is only the beginning

Ghost Stories

escaping into a fierce dawn
I spent too much time
spiraling in silence
restless in bed
remembering when I crept
out of yours
slipping into my jeans and sneakers
intense haste

when apparitions appeared
I burned my guilt in poems
swallowed salt for the memory
it was my favourite game
unlearning shame
with a glass of wine in hand
and pretending
I could kiss you anytime
or argue with your coy love
that led to my escape
in the first place

it was a mistake
not easy to learn from
I beaded them on regalia
telling the story of owls dancing
then vanishing to the ends of wants
immortal in the moment
harshly relearning
love stories are ghost stories

Real Name

you told me
your real name was grief

I sat
counting silences

the ticking clock
hiked walls

my pumping heart
like a barking dog

its growl
echoed

throughout the night
half awake

the empty hallways
were full

of insects fiddling music
grief heard in any song

Heartache

1)
my brown skin turns grey
I hear the sound of heartache
a river gushing

2)
my heart is cement
something ugly to walk on
jackhammers are tools

3)
grief is tragic art
brooding artists love to paint
flies are annoying

Roads

a solid path
dotted yellow line
division of traffic flowing
sometimes in opposite directions
other times driving towards the same
destination leading to inspiration bound by hope
cementing all roads paved by the journeys that hearts take

this was our path

Finger Painting

my skin, my skin
still reminds you
of your last lover, I can tell
by the way your fingers paint
a different frame than mine
rolling over my body
forgetting spots on my belly
that make me flinch

or when you exhale love breath
along my spine, you have forgotten
the art of creating tremors on my skin canvas
or sounds rumbling within my blood
or how loudly my skin speaks
when the sun is so close
it steams my body

it is crazy
knowing everything
beautiful has a consequence
like kissing scars, a body of wounds and reminders
old and deep enough
compelling
me to love myself
since there was a time I didn't

I still allow whispers
that escape secrets of you
that allow my skin to tremble pleasure
when you were there
with me in stark love
but sometimes, I accept things when I shouldn't
sometimes, I am too loud when I dream
twisting dreamy thoughts of you into metaphors
making truth into impressionistic art
or poetry that contemplates the human condition
because I am so good at hiding
what quakes within
so good at falling in love

with others who can't love me back
so good at being the prey
so good in addictions
and you are so good
at not committing to a completed piece of art

it's a quiver in my stomach
killing butterflies
it's understanding
how to use a body canvas in different ways
like responding to my sounds
like the way you paint my body
like the reminders left aching on my skin

Deep Breaths

we were in love in war
moving wounded
through the round horizon
empty rivers awaiting
heaven's tears

we took deep breaths
and let the wetness of war
talk to our bodies burning
beneath a hazy sunset
sure that our love would greet morning

we saw what others couldn't
and it was shameless smiling
amid the guns pointing at us
because we dared to be ourselves
despite the bullets of others

Naked Rain

naked rain
softly falling
near the last pool of light

its rhythm lulls new
language for body poetry

a saxophone drones
sleeks through silent dusk
a melodic tranquility compels
eyes to take a chance
the small twitch on lips
booms
the right moment
creating the perfect pitch
limbs respond
mellow jazz
skin whispers
licked by evening breath
provoking
belly dances
rhythmic waves
hooking hips
lapping at the pool's edge
spines curving
poetically

wild animals fever
hunger
driving
contentment
forest grown
strawberries wolfed
remnants speckling
trampled grass

salmon waiting
a sailor's sky
fades past dusk

sailing
deep blue caves
emerging
warm pools
swimming
into a swollen moon

electrified senses
exploding
never-heard-before sounds
a new language is born
naked in rain
glimmering and shining
this poem

Lay Down with Me

so I drift into
Friday night dreams
in love with love ache
your poetry breaking me
open to simple intentions

lay down with me
and let the rise
and fall of your breath
bend into my naked skin
pulsing
my dreams awake

xwexwistsín - I love you

On That Rooftop in Arequipa

it would've been so easy
to fall in love with you
on that rooftop in Arequipa
as I tried to sleep my sicknesses away

destiny—you later called it
but it was weakness and foolishness
because I don't learn so easily

realization is a dreamless voyage
oddly peaceful, still the sky rises
infinitely from my body outward
and from the streets below
the echoes of other's chatter
drifts droning nonsense
as my body ached release

obliviously, I did not know
you sat watching over me
patient as brewing wars
steady as the poet's mind
but when I opened my eyes
I saw you for the first time
soul shining softness

your hand deep in poetry
your body moving wind-like
a glass of wine
an open book

Brothers

for Guy

if there is such a thing as luck
then I can claim
I am a lucky man

we are brothers
sanctified by blood
gifted by birth

from the beginning
we understood
sameness and solidarity

the recognition of unbreakable bonds
through brotherly adoration
never taken for granted

in this time and space
we understand
unspoken respect

binding us as horsemen
thick and blue horses
galloping pavement

the rush of rodeo
the ride is never the same
and we never drift apart

we are brothers

Morning Light

I am most alive in early mornings
sipping coffee
watching the grey ache of dawn
dissolve shadows

it rained last night
air is full
lingering of cotton wood scent
dust before it turns to puddles

the tiny blue sounds of rain
dripping from the tin roof
catches my attention
I study its inconsistency

the time it takes to reach ground
morning light travelling within it
the sum of it all
says things my heart can't

For This Moment

for this moment I lay
next to you during the love hours
the night is always half awake
a perfect time to challenge
frightened flowers
that grow too slowly in the dark
to feed the hungry
or find solace in the heat of my breath

you know well
thunder whispering
low rumbling from far off
throats raw with gratitude
music arising from flushed skin
the releasing of your name, and mine
and I am yours for this moment

Mataora

for Graham Grayza Tipene

he is committed now
there is no turning back
black ash of ink embedded
deeply in his facial skin
burning needle humming
'mataora'
reminding him
that to abuse women is not to be
and so, the notice of the reason she left
makes this story infinite
men need balance and reason
women need protection and love
otherwise the sound of two breaking hearts
will be heard through ink
one of pain
one of joy

Silence

sometimes words never have to be
said between two people
expanse of meaning is understood
within the astounding silence

this is not surreal
nor disguised interpretation
because when likeminded souls link
it is endearment

Rodeo Morning

green-broke boys aroused
by the restless chill
on daybreak rodeo mornings
when the old world still sleeps
dreaming stories

in the sound of silence
birds chatter noisily in dawn
dogs bark at the far off unknown
breaking dreams

eagerness in chill
vivid minds calculating
perhaps mistakenly
thinking
they are already cowboys

bodies ablaze
burning instincts
hunger in the air
fuel aching urges

waiting for dawn's sun to be full
a time of heated passion
riding night through
from boys to men
secrets of manhood
solid in a moment's memory

dreaming silence
on daybreak rodeo mornings

Phenomena

I watch
sun's crawling rays spread
brilliance edging over the Rockies
where shadow pockets
hide in caves and crevasses

I hide
you in those places
knowing my heart beats differently
when you appear shining
blending vivid prisms
and exposure is liberating

I wait
at sun's edge
watching
for your arrival
to crawl across the Rockies each morning

Awakening

awakening is a sunrise ceremony
vulnerable and ready to greet the world
she tells the story in dawn
of devotion and pain
centuries old
like rumbling avalanches
inducing contractions
a mother's buoyant blood
breaking free
the son who can't recall the agony
only she knew
two hearts to become individuals by birthing
returning cycles
raising hands to honour
something more powerful than themselves
something that reinforces
she is alive
and has given life
a simple prayer
imploring strength for her newborn, family and clan
and even those yet to be born
and now those who have become ancestors

it is her telling
when he becomes a man the time is right
an awakening sky and shared love

a story worth telling

Inclusionary

vigorous beauty
in your old age
is worth remembering
all of you

transitioning
our youthful lust
into a lifelong journey
has solidified our reason for life

I have no regrets

Moko Kauae
for Auntie Arohanui

who would believe Auntie Arohanui's story
if it were not for Moko Kauae?

it is not easy to forget
a woman's purpose

although her journey
is easily misunderstood

so when she speaks
her words are raw power

if you do not listen
she can unearth the underworld

it has nothing to do with survival
and everything to do with birthright

Driving Slow on Sunday Morning

I believed Sunday
mornings were for worship

this day, chosen for purpose

standing in a church parking lot
the world quiet around us
ready to depart

I stared at the long road ahead
at the yellow division
realizing there are no clean lines
between heaven and earth
no doves hovering in air
or angels in choir
no streaming beams of light
to guide uncertainty

the world is full of the unexpected
like a road without signs

what was I to do
but dig deep into my pockets
searching for keys
and a renewed destination
with you hand in hand
driving slow on Sunday morning

Forever Man

for Airini and Rakuera

she saw home
when she looked into his eyes
solace
where foundations are firm
structures
familiar as her own

"you are my forever man," she said

her words
seeped into his bones
silently
his eyes did the speaking
echoing her words
he is a man after all—a forever man

Only Once

matters of the heart
are risky business

it is so easy to lose one's identity
for another's desire

but then, when the kinks are worked out
pure contentment is the gift

only once
maybe twice

Blue Collar Dudes

this ain't just a slide-in dream

hell NO!

it's live action
featuring blue collar dudes
tricks and tools
century old rhythms
'come'n get me baby'
below the hips
gay or straight
or something in between
take notice
webbing selfies
fingering
texting on android
the scent of 'hot'
facebook streaming live
youtube junkies see it all
making the apple men shine red
panting proudly
"I'm up for it!"
crowbar ready
drilling
passionate fun
entry the true north
strong and free
naughty boys
well equipped
with nice butts and essential services
construction is a manly thing

Acknowledgements

There are people in my life who stand by me regardless. I want to acknowledge and thank Sean Cranbury for his relentless support and believing that my poetic voice has value. Included in this list is my long-time friend Bette Shippam, who takes every opportunity to support and promote my poetry, and who endlessly continues to encourage me to keep writing, even though I continuously doubt myself. I thank my dear friend Natalie Clark, whose keen insights regarding poetic voice has guided this publication to completion. I want to thank my editor, Sarah de Leeuw, for her amazing insights. Finally, I am grateful to Caitlin Press for accepting this manuscript for publication.

Notes

"Cactus and Wild Roses" was included in *Introduction to Determinants of First Nations, Inuit, and Métis Peoples' Health in Canada* (Canadian Scholars, 2022)

"Imagine That!" and "Floating" were previously published in *The Salt Chuck City Review* (Aboriginal Writers Collective, 2019)

About the Author

GARRY GOTTFRIEDSON is from Kamloops, BC. He is strongly rooted in his Secwépemc cultural teachings. He holds a Master of Arts Education Degree from Simon Fraser University. In 1987, the Naropa Institute in Boulder, Colorado, awarded a Creative Writing scholarship to Gottfriedson. There, he studied under Allen Ginsberg, Marianne Faithfull and others. Gottfriedson has ten published books. He has read from his work across Canada, the United States, South America, New Zealand, Europe, and Asia. His work has been anthologized and published nationally and internationally. Currently, he works at Thompson Rivers University.